Fact Finders™

The American Colonies

The
Rhode Island Colony

by Kathleen W. Deady

Consultant:
Dr. Robert E. McCarthy
Professor of History
Providence College
Providence, Rhode Island

Capstone
press

Mankato, Minnesota

Fact Finders is published by Capstone Press,
151 Good Counsel Drive, P.O. Box 669, Mankato, Minnesota 56002.
www.capstonepress.com

Library of Congress Cataloging-in-Publication Data
Deady, Kathleen W.
    The Rhode Island colony / by Kathleen W. Deady.
    p. cm. — (Fact Finders. The American colonies)
    ISBN 0-7368-2682-3 (hardcover)
    1. Rhode Island—History—Colonial period, ca. 1600–1775—Juvenile literature.
    I. Title. II. Series: American colonies (Capstone Press)
F82.D43 2006
974.5'02—dc22   2005001878

Summary: An introduction to the history, government, economy, resources, and people of
    the Rhode Island Colony. Includes maps and charts.

Editorial Credits
Mandy Marx, editor; Jennifer Bergstrom, set designer, illustrator, and book designer;
    Bobbi J. Dey, book designer; Jo Miller, photo researcher/photo editor

Photo Credits
Cover: Color print of wharf workers measuring whale oil content in barrels,
    Corbis/Bettmann

Corbis/Bettmann, 11, 21
Getty Images Inc./Archive Photos, 5
The Granger Collection/New York, 10, 15, 19, 23, 26
National Archives and Records Administration, 27, 29 (right)
North Wind Picture Archives, 12–13, 14, 16–17, 29 (left)
Superstock, 6–7

1 2 3 4 5 6 10 09 08 07 06 05

Table of Contents

Chapter 1

Rhode Island's First People

Long before European arrival, Rhode Island was home to American Indians. The Narragansett were the most powerful group in the area. They ruled many other tribes.

Way of Life

The Narragansett lived in villages of about 100 people. Each village had a leader called a sachem. When a sachem died, a younger man in his family took over. The main leader of the people was called the grand sachem. He ruled the Narragansett and smaller tribes nearby.

Ninigret was a Narragansett ruler in the 1600s.

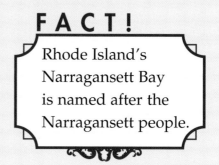

The Narragansett moved with the changes of seasons. In summer, they lived by the ocean in rounded huts called wigwams. Men fished, and women grew corn, beans, and squash. In winter, the tribe moved to the forest. There, they lived in longhouses. Men hunted wild animals. The people also ate fruits and vegetables dried from summer's harvest.

The Narragansett knew of the first English colonies. But they did not understand the English settlers' weapons and way of life. Narragansett leaders decided to avoid the English.

FACT!

Rhode Island's Narragansett Bay is named after the Narragansett people.

◀ In winter, the Narragansett made traps to catch animals.

Chapter 2

Early Settlers

Like its neighbor Massachusetts, Rhode Island was started by people wanting religious freedom. The Puritans who settled Massachusetts had fled England, where their religion was not allowed. But in the winter of 1636, Roger Williams fled Massachusetts.

Roger Williams was a young Puritan minister. He did not agree with the Puritans who ruled the Massachusetts Bay Colony. Williams preached that religion and government should be separate. He said people had the right to choose their own religion. This idea upset many Puritan leaders.

In 1763, colonial borders were set. Rhode Island was squeezed between the Puritan colonies of Massachusetts and Connecticut. ➡

The Rhode Island Colony, 1763

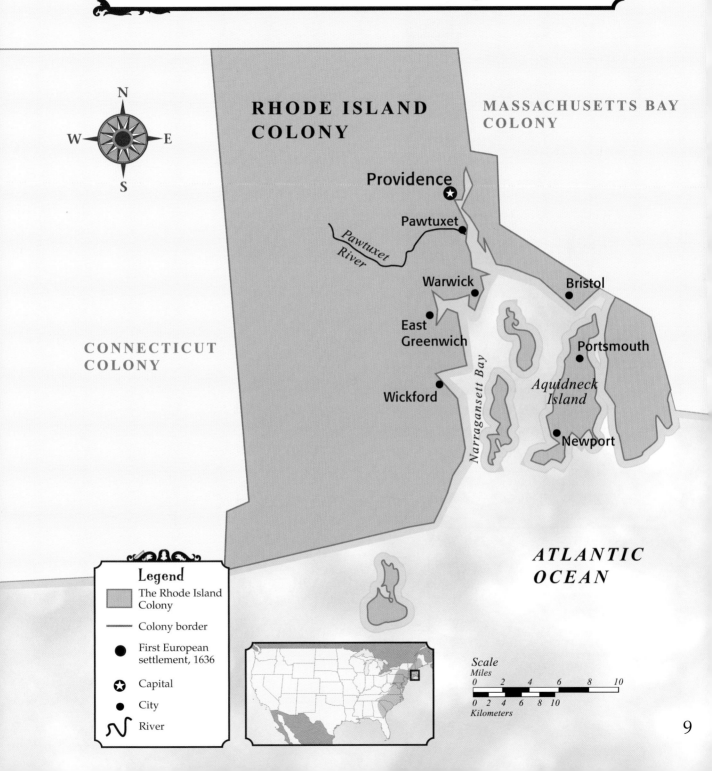

RHODE ISLAND COLONY

MASSACHUSETTS BAY COLONY

CONNECTICUT COLONY

Providence

Pawtuxet

Pawtuxet River

Warwick

Bristol

East Greenwich

Portsmouth

Wickford

Narragansett Bay

Aquidneck Island

Newport

ATLANTIC OCEAN

Legend

The Rhode Island Colony

Colony border

First European settlement, 1636

Capital

City

River

Scale
Miles
0 2 4 6 8 10
0 2 4 6 8 10
Kilometers

▲ The Narragansett helped Roger Williams.

FACT!

Anne Hutchinson was kicked out of Massachusetts for preaching. There, only men were allowed to preach. Hutchinson helped start Portsmouth, Rhode Island.

Massachusetts' Puritan leaders planned to arrest Williams and send him back to England. Williams learned of the plan and fled. He met some Narragansett Indians who took pity on him. They cared for him through the winter. In June, the Indians gave Williams land by Narragansett Bay. There, he started Providence, Rhode Island's first English settlement.

Forming a Colony

Others seeking religious freedom soon followed Williams. They began the towns of Portsmouth, Warwick, and Newport.

People of many faiths came to Rhode Island. The leaders of Massachusetts and Connecticut disliked having these people so close to their colonies. They tried to take over the new settlements.

Providence, Portsmouth, Warwick, and Newport needed legal protection. In 1663, King Charles II of England gave them a **charter**. The charter joined the towns as the colony of Rhode Island.

Rhode Island's first settlers built fences around their homes to keep animals out. ▼

~ Chapter 3 ~
Colonial Life

Rhode Island's first settlers built farms and towns in the wilderness. Daily life was filled with chores. Men built homes and cleared land to farm. Women cooked, cleaned, and raised children. Children helped their parents whenever they could. Most children learned adult tasks at a very young age.

Families produced most of their own food. Corn was the main crop. Colonists also raised animals for meat, eggs, milk, and cheese. Families that lived near Narragansett Bay fished for clams, shrimp, and other seafood.

Rhode Island farmers had to clear forests before they could plant crops.

13

⬆ For most Rhode
Island colonists,
daily life centered
around the home
and farm.

Education

Education was less important in
Rhode Island than in the rest of New
England. Other colonies used school
as a place to teach religion. But Rhode
Island did not teach one faith over
another. In 1647, Massachusetts passed
a law to start public schools. Rhode
Island was the only New England
colony that did not pass a similar law.

King Philip's War

Roger Williams worked hard to keep peace with the Narragansett. But people in other colonies had treated American Indians poorly.

In 1675, the Indian chief King Philip united many tribes against the colonists. They started King Philip's War (1675–1676). The Narragansett stayed out of the war until Massachusetts colonists attacked them. In anger, they joined the battle.

Roger Williams watched as the Narragansett burned Providence to the ground. The colonists won the war in 1676. For Williams, it was a sad victory.

▲ When the Narragansett entered the war, they attacked colonists' homes.

FACT!

King Philip was an Indian chief from the Wampanoag tribe. Many of the Indians in New England died in the war he started.

Chapter 4

Work and Trade

As the colony grew, Rhode Island's **economy** changed. In the early years, most Rhode Islanders were fishers and farmers. They caught fish and grew crops for their own needs.

By the early 1700s, some farmers owned large areas of land. These large farms were called **plantations**. Many plantations were located on the rich soil near the coast. Others were on the fertile islands in Narragansett Bay. Farmers grew corn, onions, and apples. They also sold wool and cheese. Many plantation owners bought slaves from Africa. The slaves were forced to work the farmer's land and care for the animals.

Many Rhode Island farmers had apple orchards. Apple picking was hard work that took many helpers.

17

Rhode Island Colony's Exports

Agricultural Exports
apples
cattle
corn
dairy products
onions

Industrial Export
ships

Natural Resource Exports
fish and seafood
lumber

Many Rhode Island colonists made their living from the sea. Narragansett Bay provided fishers with fish, clams, lobsters, and oysters. Colonists also hunted whales off the coast. Parts of whales were used to make candles and to light lamps. Other colonists built ships to support the fishing and whaling **industries**.

As cities in the colony grew, businesses sprang up. Merchants and craftsmen set up shops along main streets and waterfronts. Newport, Providence, and Bristol became major cities.

WHALE - NANTUCK

▲ Many Rhode Island settlers found work in coastal towns.

Wealth in Trade

By the 1760s, life for most Rhode Island colonists was tied to trade. Some colonists worked in shipping or selling goods. Others were dock workers, warehouse workers, and bookkeepers. Farmers sold goods to traders. Traders then sold goods to people in England and in other American colonies.

Chapter 5

Community and Faith

Rhode Island's first settlers had many disagreements. But these disagreements helped the colony grow. William Coddington and Anne Hutchinson helped start the town of Portsmouth. But the two of them had an argument. Coddington left to start the Rhode Island town of Newport. Samuel Gorton was another Portsmouth resident who argued with Anne Hutchinson. He left to start the town of Warwick in 1642.

Quarrels between town leaders continued for nearly 40 years. But the threat of a takeover by Massachusetts and Connecticut forced town leaders to unite.

In Rhode Island, Anne Hutchinson was free to preach about the Bible.

Government

Rhode Island's charter allowed the colonists to form their own government. Land-owning white men voted for **representatives** and a governor to make laws. This system worked so well, it went unchanged for 180 years. In 1843, white men who did not own land were also allowed to vote.

Population Growth of the Rhode Island Colony

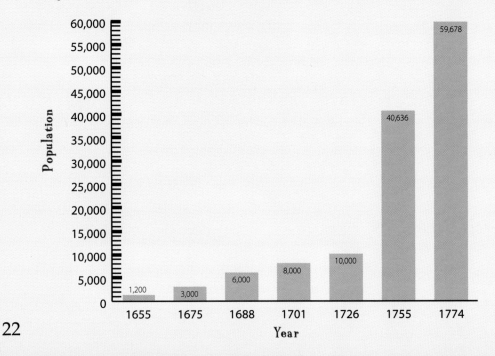

Rogue's Island

People of many faiths moved to Rhode Island. In 1639, Providence became home to the first Baptist church in America. In 1657, Quakers came to Aquidneck Island. Jewish settlers came to Newport in 1658.

New England colonists were shocked by Rhode Island's lack of religious rules. They thought settlers there were trouble-makers. Rhode Island was given the nickname "Rogue's Island."

Touro Synagogue, in Newport, was built in the 1760s. It is the oldest Jewish synagogue in the United States. ➡

Chapter 6

Becoming a State

By the 1760s, the American colonies had busy cities and large plantations. Rhode Islanders were enjoying wealth from farming and trade. At that time, Great Britain passed laws limiting trade in the colonies. Britain taxed colonists on tea, paper, and sugar.

The taxes upset many colonists. They had no say in Britain's government. For this reason, they didn't think Britain should tax them. In 1774, the colonies sent representatives to the Continental Congress. These men tried to settle matters with Great Britain. But a peaceful solution could not be found.

Rhode Island was the smallest American colony. ➡

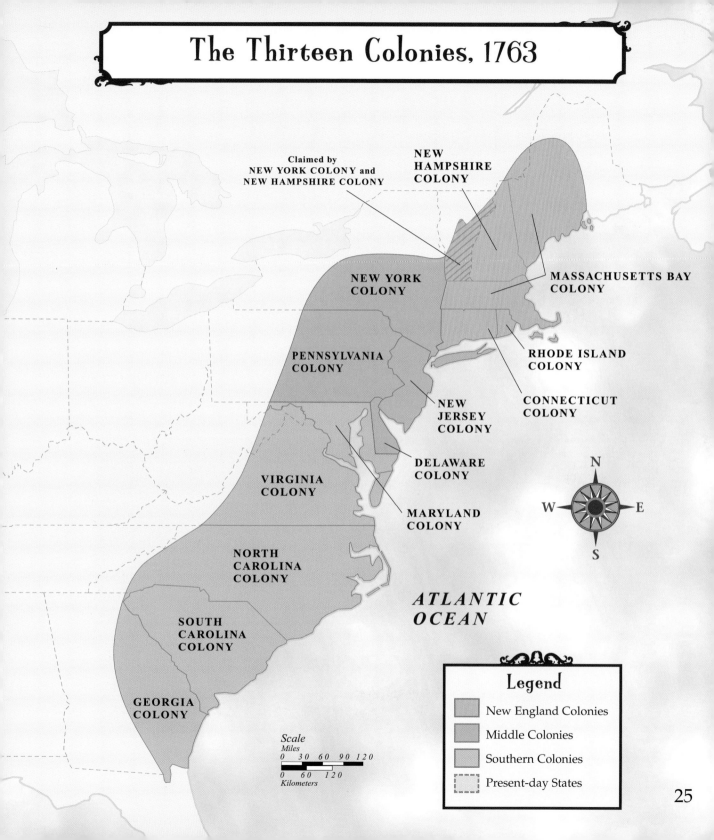

The Thirteen Colonies, 1763

Claimed by
NEW YORK COLONY and
NEW HAMPSHIRE COLONY

NEW
HAMPSHIRE
COLONY

NEW YORK
COLONY

MASSACHUSETTS BAY
COLONY

PENNSYLVANIA
COLONY

RHODE ISLAND
COLONY

CONNECTICUT
COLONY

NEW
JERSEY
COLONY

DELAWARE
COLONY

VIRGINIA
COLONY

MARYLAND
COLONY

NORTH
CAROLINA
COLONY

ATLANTIC
OCEAN

SOUTH
CAROLINA
COLONY

GEORGIA
COLONY

N
W   E
S

Scale
Miles
0   30   60   90   120

0   60   120
Kilometers

Legend

New England Colonies

Middle Colonies

Southern Colonies

Present-day States

Fight for Freedom

The Revolutionary War (1775–1783) began in 1775 in Massachusetts. Rhode Island sent soldiers to join the fight.

In July 1776, Congress approved the Declaration of **Independence**. It said that the colonies were states, free from British rule. The colonists continued to fight for that freedom in the Revolutionary War.

Many New England colonists were minutemen. They were ready to fight at all times.

The war hit home for Rhode Islanders. The British captured Newport in 1776. In 1778, Americans tried to free the city. But they lost the Battle of Rhode Island. In 1779, the British left on their own. America finally won the war in 1783.

In 1787, American leaders wrote a plan for government called the United States **Constitution**. Rhode Islanders demanded the Constitution include the Bill of Rights. This section protects the freedom of each American. On May 29, 1790, Rhode Island approved the Constitution. It was the 13th state to join the Union.

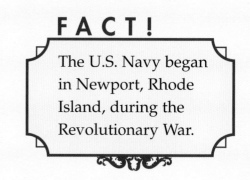

Rhode Islanders insisted the U.S. Constitution had the Bill of Rights. One of the rights it protects is freedom of religion.

FACT!

The U.S. Navy began in Newport, Rhode Island, during the Revolutionary War.

Fast Facts

Name
Rhode Island and
Providence Plantations

Location
New England

Year of Founding
1636

First Settlement
Providence

Colony's Founder
Roger Williams

Religious Faiths
Baptist, Jewish, Puritan, Quaker

Agricultural Products
Apples, corn, dairy products,
onions

Major Industries
Agriculture, fishing,
shipbuilding, trading

Population in 1774
59,678 people

Statehood
May 29, 1790
(13th state)

Time Line

1663
Rhode Island gets a charter from King Charles II of England.

1637-1642
Other towns in Rhode Island are founded, including Portsmouth, Newport, and Warwick.

1636
Roger Williams flees Massachusetts; the Narragansett give him land where he starts the town of Providence.

1763
Proclamation of 1763 sets colonial borders and provides land for American Indians.

1775
American colonies begin fight for independence from Great Britain in the Revolutionary War.

1707
An Act of Union unites England, Wales, and Scotland; they become the Kingdom of Great Britain.

1675-1676
Colonists defeat American Indians in King Philip's War.

1776-1779
Newport is occupied by the British.

1783
America wins the Revolutionary War.

1790
On May 29th, Rhode Island is the 13th state to join the United States.

1776
Declaration of Independence is approved in July.

Glossary

charter (CHAR-tur)—an official document that grants permission to create a colony and provides for a government

constitution (kon-stuh-TOO-shuhn)—the written system of laws in a state or country that state the rights of the people and the powers of the government

economy (e-KON-uh-mee)—the way a colony or government runs its business, trade, and spending

independence (in-di-PEN-duhnss)—being free from the control of other people

industry (IN-duh-stree)—a branch of business or trade

plantation (plan-TAY-shuhn)—a large farm where crops, such as coffee, tea, tobacco, and cotton, are grown

representative (rep-ri-ZEN-tuh-tiv)—someone who is chosen to speak or act for others

Internet Sites

FactHound offers a safe, fun way to find Internet sites related to this book. All of the sites on FactHound have been researched by our staff.

Here's how:

1. Visit *www.facthound.com*
2. Type in this special code **0736826823** for age-appropriate sites. Or enter a search word related to this book for a more general search.
3. Click on the **Fetch It** button.

FactHound will fetch the best sites for you!

Read More

Raum, Elizabeth. *Roger Williams*. American Lives. Chicago: Heinemann, 2005.

Somervill, Barbara A. *The Rhode Island Colony*. Our Thirteen Colonies. Chanhassen, Minn.: Child's World, 2003.

Whitehurst, Susan. *The Colony of Rhode Island*. The Library of the Thirteen Colonies and the Lost Colony. New York: PowerKids Press, 2000.

Index